To my parents,
Myrtle Palo and John W. Palo,
who opened all the doors of wonder they could
in our little corner of the world,
with thanks and love

PUBLISHER'S NOTE

Because finely crafted hymn texts have a poetic integrity of their own, Susan Palo Cherwien's hymns appear in text form in the first section of this volume. To enable their use by congregations, most of the hymns are also presented with music (accompaniments beginning on page 45, melody lines with complete texts beginning on page 89).

In addition to several widely used tunes, a number of new tunes by several noted composers are included in this collection. Some of these were commissioned, along with the texts, for particular occasions; in other cases the author wrote a text with a particular tune in mind. These are not intended to be exclusive pairings, however. Composers are invited to let these hymn texts inspire other melodies and musical settings for congregation, soloist, or choir.

CONTENTS

FOREWORD

Paul Westermeyer

If you are among those who long for hymns that are rich in language, vivid in image, and sturdy in content, this is a book that will give you reason for rejoicing. Here are texts crafted with thoughtful care, worth the time and effort of those who will sing them. While accessible on first singing, these hymns bear repetition because they probe beneath the surface to deep currents of life and meaning.

Singing—and reading—the hymns themselves will yield the best understanding of them. Rather than analyze or explain them, let me make some general observations.

First, authors' notes on the background of particular hymns are always helpful. They invariably give insights into the writing that would not be otherwise available. Collections of an author's hymns are valuable sources for this information. But good hymns always transcend the occasions of their composition. These hymns do that. Whether you know their origins or not, they stand as expressions of the faith able to be sung by congregations in many times and places.

Second, the character of these hymns as *corporate* expressions of faith for Christian congregations is important to note. Poets in our period are encouraged to express an individual and idiosyncratic character. Good hymn writers are rare because they have a quite different task— namely, to articulate the faith of the church in such a way that an assembly will be able to sing what it needs to express. The good hymn writer gives the congregation its voice and is representative, not idiosyncratic. Susan Palo Cherwien's hymns have that representative character.

Third, to be representative means voicing the song of the church in our idioms, not past ones. Those hymns of the past that we still sing with lively vigor and gratefulness are from writers who spoke with honesty and integrity in their periods. They may have been influenced and inspired by past forms, but they imbued these forms with the concerns and expressions of their time and place. Good writers today do no less. In Susan Palo Cherwien's hymns you will note many themes from our period, always set in a Christocentric context and expressed in a remarkable array of meters and rhyme schemes.

Fourth, you will also note that fear and trembling are here. When the Christian church is true to its mission, it lives in and seeks to respond to the world with loving grace, but it never becomes the world. It has another message which paradoxically affirms the world's being by standing against its ingrown perversions. Our period sometimes tends to perceive God as a celestial puppy dog for our play rather than Source of all sources, Being of all beings, Spirit behind spirit. That is why we are tempted to omit fear and trembling, not to mention careful crafting. This book points to the church's deeper and more potent instincts. Its texts are not afraid to stand in awe, nor to seek the finest art to express the inexpressible.

Finally, these texts lead where doxological awe always leads—to serving the world by living gratefully and freely into the future. Along that journey, may hymns like this move us:

Shine your future on this place,
Enlighten every guest,
That through us stream your holiness...

Rise, remember well the future
God has called us to receive...

Service be our sure vocation,
Courage be our daily breath;
Mercy be our destination...
Alleluia.

HYMNS

A RAM'S HORN BLASTING BARREN HILLS

A ram's horn blasting barren hills,
The bells which sleeping city prod,
Call worship to the waking world:
Laud your God.

In praise the voices vibrant rise
As one, the great enlightened crowd—
Diversity in unison,
Clothed in cloud.

Enheartened by the Spirit-song,
And healed, like Saul, by godly guest,
We sing, we soar, we rise to live,
Blessing blest.

Great God, who gave us mystery,
Who clothed the stars in song divine,
Be present in our harmony—
Sign in sine.

AS THE DARK AWAITS THE DAWN

As the dark awaits the dawn,
So we await your light.
O Star of promise, scatter night,
Loving bright, loving bright,
Till shades of fear are gone.

As the blue expectant hour
Before the silvering skies,
We long to see your day arise,
Whole and wise, whole and wise,
O lucent Morning Star.

As the moon reflects the sun
Until the night's decrease,
May we your healing light release,
Living peace, living peace,
Unto your holy dawn.

Shine your future on this place,
Enlighten every guest,
That through us stream your holiness,
Bright and blest, bright and blest;
Come dawn, O Sun of grace.

BELOVED, GOD'S CHOSEN

Beloved, God's chosen,
Put on as a garment
Compassion, forgiveness, and goodness of heart.
Above all, before all,
Let love be your raiment
That binds into one every dissonant part.

Within, call forth Wisdom,
To dwell in you richly;
Let peace rule your hearts, and that peace be of Christ.
And from the heart's chamber,
Beloved and holy,
Let singing thanksgiving to God ever rise.

Beloved, God's chosen,
Put on as a garment
Compassion, forgiveness, and goodness of heart.
Above all, before all,
Let love be your raiment
That binds into one every dissonant part.

BLESSING BE AND GLORY

Blessing be and glory to the Living One,
Who in empty tomb and rising is made known;
God on earth, and, lo, the splendid mystery:
God on earth, and death can claim no victory.

Power and dominion to the Faithful One,
Who in wounds and peace at evening is made known:
God in Christ, and grace is loosed that all may be
Resurrected, joyful people, whole and free.

Wisdom and thanksgiving to the Risen One,
Who in bread and fish at dawning is made known:
God in Christ, and mortals can courageously
Live and love undaunted by mortality.

Honor be and might unto the Holy One,
Who in bread and wine and sharing is made known:
God in Christ in us, so that the world may see
In all days the splendor of divinity.

BRIGHT JOINING
Meditations on the Cross

Bright joining of godly and human
Eternity coupling with present
Embracing clear light and thick darkness
Blest cross, star announcing the Savior.

Blest union of evil and holy
Absorbing and willing transforming
Embracing the pain of the cosmos
Blest cross, outstretched arms of the Savior.

Grand juncture of dying and living
A drowning deep blue into newness
Embracing Christ's death and arising
Blest cross, sign anointing our forehead.

Great fusion of body and spirit
In exile yet living the promise
Embracing life's daily small dying
Blest cross, faith traced hand upon body.

Bright bonding of matter and power
Enfolding, expelling, igniting
Embracing deep space and small fragment
Blest cross, cosmic arms of the Savior.

CHRIST, BURNING WISDOM

Christ, burning Wisdom,
Burn in us brightly,
Lumine us lovely,
So that your people,
Filled with the Holy,
Lighten the darkness.

Christ, gentle River,
Flow in us meekly,
Drown us in mercy,
So that your people,
Empty of clinging,
Fill with your newness.

Christ, Bread of heaven,
Rise in us sweetly,
Fill us with beauty,
So that your people
With your compassion
Leaven creation.

Christ, living Presence,
Breathe in us deeply,
Sigh through us wholly,
So that your people,
Filled with your fragrance,
Live from your Spirit.

Christ, the illuming,
Christ, the forgiving,
Christ, the upraising,
Christ, the inspiring:
All that has being
Joys in your glory.

CHRIST IS THE LIFE

Christ is the life of all that is,
God's pure creative Word,
Whose power beyond and through all space
The worlds to Being stirred.
Christ is the life beyond all time,
Creation's birth and breath,
Whose labor brings all things to be
And brings all things to death.

Christ is the death of all that is,
A broad and beckoning tomb,
Who welcomes us from well-worn ways
To darkness of the womb.
Christ is the death, the sinking down
Past all desire and fear,
Whose promise in the gentle dark
Bids newness to appear.

Christ is the death of all that is,
A bright, consuming fire,
Whose flames require our prior self
As kindling for the pyre.
Christ is the death of dusty days
Of uncreative strife,
For out from fire we tread upon
The threshold of new life.

Christ is the life of all that is,
Beginning and the End;
Creative force, most peaceful death,
Transforming burning brand.
Christ is the life, in whose wise love
Creation lives and dies
And thus forevermore shall bless
The Source, the living Christ.

CREATOR GOD, WHO GAVE US LIFE

Creator God, who gave us life,
Who breathed us into song,
Who set in us creative drive,
From whom our utmost dreams derive,
To whom all arts belong:

Infuse us with your fertile grace
And consecrate our art;
Bring springtime to our wilderness
Where void and talent interface
And power to us impart;

That through your artists, thus inspired,
All barrenness may flee;
All hearts and minds be opened wide
And minds thus opened glimpse inside
Your love and majesty.

DAY OF ARISING

Day of arising,
Christ on the roadway,
Unknown companion
Walks with his own.
When they invite him,
As fades the first day,
And bread is broken,
Christ is made known.

When we are walking,
Doubtful and dreading,
Blinded by sadness,
Slowness of heart,
Yet Christ walks with us
Ever awaiting
Our invitation:
Stay, do not part.

Lo, I am with you,
Jesus has spoken.
This is Christ's promise,
This is Christ's sign:
When the church gathers,
When bread is broken,
There Christ is with us
In bread and wine.

Christ, our companion,
Hope for the journey,
Bread of compassion,
Open our eyes.
Grant us your vision,
Set all hearts burning
That all creation
With you may rise.

FROM LOVING HANDS

From loving hands your grace has poured
And blessed and formed the living world:
From sound and fir to farm and hill
Your earthen works reveal you still.
All glory be to God.

From mount to shore, O Christ, you bless
The home of welcome, haven, rest,
Where door and hearth and cup and board
Receive all in your name, O Lord.
All glory be to God.

Within each home, O Spirit, tend
The parent hands that soothe and mend,
Whose holding, feeding, guiding heal
And to the child your truth reveal.
All glory be to God.

From sun to sun, from stone to green,
Your gracious presence may be seen,
Not housed in past or distant lands,
But in the work of loving hands.
All glory be to God.

GLORY TO YOU, GOD

Glory to you, God, for yours is the earth;
yours is the promise, the blessing, the birth.
Ours the rejoicing for Word given frame;
ours the thanksgiving to your holy name.
Ours be the telling of deeds greatly done;
yours be the glory, O God, yours alone.

Glory to you, God, for yours is the earth;
yours the hosannas, the dying, rebirth.
Ours the rejoicing for nature reclaimed;
ours the thanksgiving to your holy name.
Ours be the telling of deeds greatly done;
yours be the glory, O God, yours alone.

Glory to you, God, for yours is the earth;
yours the anointing, the radiant worth.
Ours the rejoicing for spirits aflame;
ours the thanksgiving to your holy name.
Ours be the telling of deeds greatly done;
yours be the glory, O God, yours alone.

GOD HAS CALLED US

God has called us:
and how can we but raise
our voices, echoing God's praise?
God has called us:
and let us answer with our lives.

God has changed us:
and how can we but live
as servants of the Spirit's gift?
God has changed us:
and let us worship with our lives.

God has charged us:
and how can we but ask
for wisdom for the Christly task?
God has charged us:
and let us labor with our lives.

God has called us:
and how can we but raise
our voices, echoing God's praise?
God has called us:
and let us answer with our lives.

HOLY WOMAN, GRACEFUL GIVER

Holy woman, graceful giver,
Prophet, servant, and believer,
Woman with the ointment jar,
Rose up near the time appointed,
Broke the seal, Christ's head anointed
For the coming fatal hour.

Like the vessel, we are broken;
Like the ointment, we are token
Of God's loving unto death;
Like the woman, we are serving;
Like the scolders, ill deserving
Such a rich, forgiving faith.

In these jars is hidden treasure,
Costly fragrance, Christly pleasure,
Like the Christ, first from the dead,
Broken for creation's wholeness,
Poured out for its coming fullness,
Prophet, Servant, Hope, and Head.

Holy woman, costly treasure,
With the jar of alabaster,
Shows the hidden gift we are;
Therefore let us as Christ's servants
Hold our sister in remembrance,
Woman with the ointment jar.

IN DEEPEST NIGHT

In deepest night, in darkest days,
When harps are hung, no songs we raise,
When silence must suffice as praise,
Yet sounding in us quietly
There is the song of God.

When friend was lost, when love deceived,
Dear Jesus wept, God was bereaved;
So with us in our grief God grieves,
And round about us mournfully
There are the tears of God.

When through the waters winds our path,
Around us pain, around us death,
Deep calls to deep, a saving breath,
And found beside us faithfully
There is the love of God.

IN SACRED MANNER

In sacred manner may we walk
Upon the fair and loving earth,
In beauty move, in beauty love
The living round that brought us birth.
We stand on holy ground.
We stand on holy ground.

In sacred manner may we see
The luminous and loving stars,
With wonder and with awe behold
Their ever-new creative powers.
The heavens show us God.
The heavens show us God.

In sacred manner may we touch
The suspirant and loving green,
Give honor and give gratitude
For shade, for bloom, for gift unseen.
The trees shall shout for joy.
The trees shall shout for joy.

In sacred manner may we hear
The pounding waves, the searing fire,
The rushing wind, the singing night,
The forest hymn, the loving choir.
The morning stars shall sing.
The morning stars shall sing.

In sacred manner may we live
Among the wise and loving ones,
Sit humbly, as at sages' feet,
By four-legged, finned and feathered ones.
The animals will teach.
The animals will teach.

In sacred manner may we walk
Upon the fair and loving earth,
In beauty move, in beauty love
The living round that brought us birth.
We stand on holy ground.
We stand on holy ground.

IN THE DESERT, ON GOD'S MOUNTAIN

In the desert, on God's mountain,
Moses saw the bush aflame,
Wondered at the fiery foliage,
Heard the crackling call his name.
May we notice bushes burning;
May we wonder at the flame.

On Mount Horeb Moses halted,
Stood unshod on holy ground,
Felt the pulsing of God's presence,
Sensed the holiness around.
May we stop amid life's labor;
May we honor holy ground.

I AM THAT I AM have called you,
Spoke the incandescent voice.
Moses felt the message searing
To the heart of will and choice.
May we pause to answer summons;
May we hear God's burning voice.

Moses hid his face in terror,
Offered his objections four:
Doubt of worth and doubt of talent,
Lack of trust and lack of lore.
May we set aside excuses;
May we take the task before.

Later in the wild of Sinai,
From another mountain height,
Bringing promise to his people,
Moses shone with God's own light.
May we, not consumed, yet burning,
Guide all to the mountain height.

Far from deserts, far from mountains,
Yearns a bound humanity.
Filled with fire of holy grounding,
Burning bushes may we be,
Drawing all to God's bright presence—
Beacons of divinity.

IN THE FAIR MORNING

In the fair morning,
Soft sun arising,
Bringing spice, expecting death,
We seek the body,
Sadness and silence,
And hear an angel voice instead:
Fear not, O people!
You seek your Jesus;
God has acted, do not fear.
Seek him in living,
Seek him in loving,
But in this grave—he is not here.

Why stand there weeping?
Why weep in sorrow?
Jesus lives, and fear has fled.
Roll away sadness,
View this arising:
Jesus is raised, and death is dead.
Bow not your faces,
Rise up in wonder,
Christ awaits you on the way;
In the fair morning,
Bright sun arising,
Christ waits to greet you to the day.

O BLESSED SPRING

O blessed spring, where Word and sign
Embrace us into Christ the Vine:
Here Christ enjoins each one to be
A branch of this life-giving Tree.

Through summer heat of youthful years,
Uncertain faith, rebellious tears,
Sustained by Christ's infusing rain,
The boughs will shout for joy again.

When autumn cools and youth is cold,
When limbs their heavy harvest hold,
Then through us, warm, the Christ will move
With gifts of beauty, wisdom, love.

As winter comes, as winters must,
We breathe our last, return to dust;
Still held in Christ, our souls take wing
And trust the promise of the spring.

Christ, holy Vine, Christ, living Tree,
Be praised for this blest mystery:
That Word and water thus revive
And join us to your Tree of Life.

O GRANT US, CHRIST, A DEEP HUMILITY

O grant us, Christ, a deep humility,
So that your church a kneeling church may be:
  Kneeling in wonder with the shepherd band,
  Kneeling in beauty, ointment jar in hand,
  Kneeling in dust to write forgiven sins,
  Kneeling in love to wash the feet of friends.

O grant us, Christ, a joyous charity,
So that your church a loving church may be:
  Loving with hands that hold hands never held,
  Loving with tears from deep compassion welled,
  Loving with bread to break, to bless, to share,
  Loving with heart of silent pain and prayer.

O grant us, Christ, a pure simplicity,
So that your church a praying church may be:
  Praying with hands that tend and care and bless,
  Praying with voice alive with thankfulness,
  Praying with eyes that recognize the Christ,
  Praying with heart abrim with Paradise.

Your church, O Christ, with holiness imbue,
So that the church transfigure into you;
  That, drawn into your great and mystic throng
  And focused in one Body and one song,
  We see the reign of God come far and broad
  And kneel before the majesty of God.

O SACRED RIVER

O sacred River, from whose flow
The stars, the seas, the cells were cast,
Whose playful patterns brought to life
The surging earth, the heavens vast:
      Murmur in us, that we know
      That you still within us flow.

O sacred Darkness, from whose night
The seed may flower, the spirit, bloom,
Whose warm embraces brought to pass
Creation's fruit, an empty tomb:
      To your shadow us invite
      That we may not shun the night.

O sacred Beauty, from whose Word
The oceans blast, the tempests play,
Whose holy palette brought to light
The crimson dawn, translucent day:
      Wake in us the artist surd
      That we manifest your Word.

O sacred Banquet, from whose love
The thirsty drink, the hungry fare,
Whose invitation brought to feast
The image lost, the heart's despair:
      To compassion may we move
      That all feast upon your love.

O SEA, MYSTIC SOURCE

O Sea, mystic Source,
Relentless and fathomless,
All streams run to you.

O River, fair Stream,
O earth-bounded Wanderer,
You seek the low place.

O Rain, soaring Mist,
Osmotic and life-giving,
Your form, the vessel's.

O Water, O Life,
O Fountain and Origin,
Have mercy on us.

RICH IN PROMISE

Rich in promise, rich in present,
Dry as dust and desert sand,
Buried in the potent land,
Deep and dark the grain lies dormant:
  Behold, God does a new thing,
  Through death God brings new life.

Running river in the desert,
Water meets the wilderness,
Transformation, more from less,
Swollen seed sends newness skyward:
  Behold, God does a new thing,
  Through death God brings new life.

Parable of grain and greening,
Paradox of death and birth,
Story of our wait in earth
For the sacramental raining:
  Behold, God does a new thing,
  Through death God brings new life.

So we move from seed to ripeness,
So we move from grain to green,
Letting go of what has been,
We embody God's great promise:
  Behold, God does a new thing,
  Through death God brings new life.

RISE, O CHURCH, LIKE CHRIST ARISEN

Rise, O church, like Christ arisen,
From this meal of love and grace;
May we through such love envision
Whose we are, and whose, our praise.
Alleluia, alleluia:
God, the wonder of our days.

Rise, transformed, and choose to follow
After Christ, though wounded, whole;
Broken, shared, our lives are hallowed
To release and to console.
Alleluia, alleluia:
Christ, our present, past, and goal.

Rise, remember well the future
God has called us to receive;
Present by God's loving nurture,
Spirited then let us live.
Alleluia, alleluia:
Spirit, grace by whom we live.

Service be our sure vocation;
Courage be our daily breath;
Mercy be our destination
From this day and unto death.
Alleluia, alleluia:
Rise, O church, a living faith.

SWEET COMING FOR WHICH WE LONG

Sweet coming for which we long:
Soft coming of star-voiced Child;
Still coming in fragrant meal;
Swift coming for wondrous weal.
Sure coming, both hope and trial;
Soon coming, our wistful song.

TEACH US TO SEEK

Teach us to seek on earth the lowest place,
To sit at table with the hungry poor,
To beg in noontide sun the crust of bread,
Receive as guest the gift into our hand;
For Love sought out the place of humble birth
That humble kindness mark our life on earth.
   Grant love, O God; grant love, O God,
   That humble kindness mark our life on earth.

Teach us to mourn with those whom sword has pierced,
With them to laugh when celebration flows;
Teach us to dance around the foreign fire,
To feel the warmth, to join the circled throng;
For Truth broke bread with peasant and with priest
To change our rending fear into a feast.
   Grant truth, O God; grant truth, O God,
   To change our rending fear into a feast.

Teach us to see in all whom you have made
The living image of the loving God,
And as a host see that all hands are filled
Before we from the table take and eat;
For Wisdom came and cried disparity
That greed may cede to good and charity.
   Grant wisdom, God; grant wisdom, God,
   That greed may cede to good and charity.

Teach us to live the underlying One;
Teach us to love the other without goal;
Teach us to lose the fear that does not know;
Teach us to leave the clutching of life's good;
For Peace freed us long hence from fear and hell
To stop the raging war upon ourselves.
   Grant peace in us; grant peace in us
   To stop the raging war upon ourselves.

THE JOURNEY WAS CHOSEN

The journey was chosen
when water was poured,
when head was anointed
and priesthood, restored;
The journey was chosen
when, brought to the Lord,
we rose, brought from death
into life.

The journey is strengthened
when, called as a guest,
we share bread and vintage,
God's royal repast;
The journey is strengthened:
we rise, fed and blest,
as those brought from death
into life.

The journey is holy:
to union with Christ,
in service and justice
and self-sacrifice;
The journey is holy,
transforming and wise
for those brought from death
into life.

Come, all, to the waters,
you thirsty, you spare;
Come, all, to the table,
encounter Christ there;
Come, all, on the journey
of covenant, where
all rise, brought from death
into life.

WE SING THE ONE GOD

We sing the one God, whose journey we claim
As children of story and heirs of the flame:
God molded us, married us, called us to come,
And set in us yearning to find our way home.
We journey in story, profound as the sea,
Descendants and friends of a great company:

    To emptiness, void, God's energy came—
    A burst of idea, a great ball of flame:
    Fused beauty and order and fired us of clay.
    Creation creator creates yet today:
    The canyons, the creatures, the daylight, the dark,
    All spiraling out from the same holy spark.

    To exiles of old, God's messenger came—
    A pillar of cloud and a column of flame,
    To lead them to promise, a covenant's dawn.
    And now in this people, the journey goes on:
    Hand visible clasping invisible hand,
    As countless as stars and unnumbered as sand.

    To faithful of old, God's hurricane came—
    A roaring, a tingling, and bright tongues of flame
    That filled them with passion, the Spirit of God.
    And now in that Spirit, the church burns abroad:
    So loved into being, the church then avows
    A life lived on fire as Christ's passionate Spouse.

O God, the one God, unnameable Name,
Who formed us in wisdom and sparked us to flame,
We join in procession across time and space
And share in your story in this age and place.
All praise be to you, for you call us to come:
Our Maker, Deliverer, Lover, and Home.

HYMNS WITH
ACCOMPANIMENT

A RAM'S HORN BLASTING BARREN HILLS

1 A ram's horn blast-ing bar-ren hills, the bells which sleep-ing cit - y
2 In praise the voic - es vi - brant rise as one, the great en-light-ened
3 En - heart - ened by the Spir-it - song, and healed, like Saul, by god - ly
4 Great God, who gave us mys-ter - y, who clothed the stars in song di -

prod, call wor - ship to the wak-ing world: Laud
crowd— di - ver - si - ty in u - ni - son, clothed
guest, we sing, we soar, we rise to live, bless -
vine, be pres - ent in our har-mo - ny— sign

1-3

your God.
in cloud.
ing blest.

4

in

sine.

Text: Susan Palo Cherwien
Music: Janet Hill
Text © 1987 Susan Palo Cherwien, admin. Augsburg Fortress
Music © 1997 Augsburg Fortress

SIGN IN SINE
8 8 8 3

AS THE DARK AWAITS THE DAWN

1 As the dark a - waits the dawn,
  blue ex - pec - tant hour
  moon re - flects the sun
  fu - ture on this place,

so we a - wait your light.
be - fore the sil - v'ring skies,
un - til the night's de - crease,
en - light - en ev - 'ry guest,

O Star of prom - ise, scat - ter night, lov - ing
we long to see your day a - rise, whole and
may we your heal - ing light re - lease, liv - ing
that through us stream your ho - li - ness, bright and

bright,   lov - ing   bright,   till   shades   of
wise,   whole and   wise,   O   lu - cent
peace,   liv - ing   peace,   un - to   your
blest,   bright and   blest;   come dawn,   O

1-3

fear   are   gone.
Morn - ing   Star.
ho - ly   dawn.
Sun   of

4

2 As   the
3 As   the
4 Shine   your
          grace.

Text: Susan Palo Cherwien
Music: Carl Schalk
Text © 1996 Susan Palo Cherwien, admin. Augsburg Fortress
Music © 1997 Augsburg Fortress

LUCENT
7 6 8 6 6

BELOVED, GOD'S CHOSEN

bove all, be - fore all, let love be your rai - ment that
from the heart's cham - ber, be - lov - ed and ho - ly, let
bove all, be - fore all, let love be your rai - ment that

binds in - to one ev - 'ry dis - so - nant part.
sing - ing thanks - giv - ing to God ev - er rise.
binds in - to one ev - 'ry dis - so - nant part.

Last time

rit.

Text: Susan Palo Cherwien
Music: Robert A. Hobby
Text © 1994 Susan Palo Cherwien, admin. Augsburg Fortress
Music © 1997 Augsburg Fortress

ANDREW'S SONG
6 6 11 D

BLESSING BE AND GLORY

1 Bless - ing be and glo - ry to the Liv - ing One,
2 Pow - er and do - min - ion to the Faith - ful One,
3 Wis - dom and thanks - giv - ing to the Ris - en One,
4 Hon - or be and might un - to the Ho - ly One,

who in emp - ty tomb and ris - ing is made known;
who in wounds and peace at eve - ning is made known:
who in bread and fish at dawn - ing is made known:
who in bread and wine and shar - ing is made known:

God on earth, and, lo, the splen - did mys - ter - y:
God in Christ, and grace is loosed that all may be
God in Christ, and mor - tals can cou - ra - geous - ly
God in Christ in us, so that the world may see

God on earth, and death can claim no vic - to - ry.
res - ur - rect - ed, joy - ful peo - ple, whole and free.
live and love un - daunt - ed by mor - tal - i - ty.
in all days the splen - dor of di - vin - i - ty.

Text: Susan Palo Cherwien
Music: French carol
Text © 1995 Susan Palo Cherwien, admin. Augsburg Fortress

NOUS ALLONS
11 11 11 11

CHRIST, BURNING WISDOM

1 Christ, burn-ing Wis - dom, burn in us bright - ly,
2 Christ, gen - tle Riv - er, flow in us meek - ly,
3 Christ, Bread of heav - en, rise in us sweet - ly,
4 Christ, liv - ing Pres - ence, breathe in us deep - ly,
5 Christ, the il - lum - ing, Christ, the for - giv - ing,

lu - mine us love - ly, so that your peo - ple,
drown us in mer - cy, so that your peo - ple,
fill us with beau - ty, so that your peo - ple
sigh through us whol - ly, so that your peo - ple,
Christ, the up - rais - ing, Christ, the in - spir - ing:

filled with the Ho - ly, light - en the dark - ness.
emp - ty of cling - ing, fill with your new - ness.
with your com - pas - sion leav - en cre - a - tion.
filled with your fra - grance, live from your Spir - it.
all that has be - ing joys in your glo - ry.

Text: Susan Palo Cherwien
Music: Janet Hill
Text © 1994 Susan Palo Cherwien, admin. Augsburg Fortress
Music © 1997 Augsburg Fortress

TAUNTON GAP
5 5 5 5 5 5

CHRIST IS THE LIFE

1 Christ is the life of all that is, God's pure cre - a - tive Word,
2 Christ is the death of all that is, a broad and beck- 'ning tomb,
3 Christ is the death of all that is, a bright, con - sum - ing fire,
4 Christ is the life of all that is, Be - gin - ning and the End;

whose pow'r be - yond and through all space the worlds to Be - ing stirred.
who wel - comes us from well- worn ways to dark- ness of the womb.
whose flames re - quire our pri - or self as kin - dling for the pyre.
cre - a - tive force, most peace - ful death, trans- form - ing burn - ing brand.

Christ is the life be - yond all time, cre - a - tion's birth and breath,
Christ is the death, the sink - ing down past all de - sire and fear,
Christ is the death of dust - y days of un - cre - a - tive strife,
Christ is the life, in whose wise love cre - a - tion lives and dies

whose la - bor brings all things to be and brings all things to death.
whose prom- ise in the gen - tle dark bids new- ness to ap - pear.
for out from fire we tread up - on the thresh- old of new life.
and thus for - ev - er - more shall bless the Source, the liv - ing Christ.

Text: Susan Palo Cherwien
Music: English melody, arr. Ralph Vaughan Williams
Text © 1989 Susan Palo Cherwien, admin. Augsburg Fortress

KINGSFOLD
C M D

CREATOR GOD, WHO GAVE US LIFE

1 Cre - a - tor God, who gave us life, who breathed us in - to
2 In - fuse us with your fer - tile grace and con - se - crate our
3 That through your art - ists, thus in - spired, all bar - ren - ness may

song, who set in us cre - a - tive drive, from whom our ut - most
art; bring spring - time to our wil - der - ness where void and tal - ent
flee; all hearts and minds be o - pened wide and minds thus o - pened

dreams de - rive, to whom all arts be - long, to whom all arts be - long:
in - ter - face and pow'r to us im - part, and pow'r to us im - part;
glimpse in - side your love and maj - es - ty, your love and maj - es - ty.

Text: Susan Palo Cherwien
Music: C. Hubert H. Parry
Text © 1987 Susan Palo Cherwien, admin. Augsburg Fortress

REPTON
86886

DAY OF ARISING

1 Day of a - ris - ing, Christ on the road - way,
2 When we are walk - ing, doubt - ful and dread - ing,
3 Lo, I am with you, Je - sus has spo - ken.
4 Christ, our com - pan - ion, hope for the jour - ney,

un - known com - pan - ion walks with his own.
blind - ed by sad - ness, slow - ness of heart,
This is Christ's prom - ise, this is Christ's sign:
bread of com - pas - sion, o - pen our eyes.

When they in - vite him, as fades the first day,
yet Christ walks with us ev - er a - wait - ing
when the church gath - ers, when bread is bro - ken,
Grant us your vi - sion, set all hearts burn - ing

and bread is bro - ken, Christ is made known.
our in - vi - ta - tion: Stay, do not part.
there Christ is with us in bread and wine.
that all cre - a - tion with you may rise.

Text: Susan Palo Cherwien
Music: Gaelic melody
Text © 1996 Susan Palo Cherwien, admin. Augsburg Fortress

BUNESSAN
5 5 5 4 D

FROM LOVING HANDS

1 From lov-ing hands your grace has poured and
2 From mount to shore, O Christ, you bless the
3 With-in each home, O Spir-it, tend the
4 From sun to sun, from stone to green, your

blessed and formed the liv-ing world: from sound and fir to
home of wel-come, ha-ven, rest, where door and hearth and
par-ent hands that soothe and mend, whose hold-ing, feed-ing,
gra-cious pres-ence may be seen, not housed in past or

farm and hill your earth-en works re-veal you still. All
cup and board re-ceive all in your name, O Lord. All
guid-ing heal and to the child your truth re-veal. All
dis-tant lands, but in the work of lov-ing hands. All

glo-ry be to God.
glo-ry be to God.
glo-ry be to God.

glo-ry be to God.

Text: Susan Palo Cherwien
Music: David Cherwien
Text © 1997 Susan Palo Cherwien, admin. Augsburg Fortress
Music © 1997 Augsburg Fortress

TORVEND
8 8 8 8 6

GLORY TO YOU, GOD

1 Glo-ry to you, God, for yours is the earth;
2 Glo-ry to you, God, for yours is the earth;
3 Glo-ry to you, God, for yours is the earth;

yours is the prom - ise, the bless-ing, the birth.
yours the ho - san - nas, the dy - ing, re - birth.
yours the a - noint-ing, the ra - di - ant worth.

Ours the re - joic - ing for Word giv-en frame;
Ours the re - joic - ing for na - ture re - claimed;
Ours the re - joic - ing for spir-its a - flame;

ours the thanks-giv - ing to your ho-ly name.

Ours be the tell - ing of deeds great-ly done;

yours be the glo - ry, O God, yours a - lone.

Text: Susan Palo Cherwien
Music: J. Bert Carlson
© 1995 Augsburg Fortress

YOURS ALONE
10 10 10 10 10 10

GOD HAS CALLED US

1 God has called us: and how can we but
2 God has changed us: and how can we but
3 God has charged us: and how can we but
4 God has called us: and how can we but

raise our voic - es, ech - o - ing God's praise? God has
live as ser - vants of the Spir - it's gift? God has
ask for wis - dom for the Christ - ly task? God has
raise our voic - es, ech - o - ing God's praise? God has

called us: and let us an - swer with our lives.
changed us: and let us wor - ship with our lives.
charged us: and let us la - bor with our lives.
called us: and let us an - swer with our lives.

Text: Susan Palo Cherwien
Music: David Cherwien
Text © 1994 Susan Palo Cherwien, admin. Augsburg Fortress
Music © 1996 Concordia Publishing House, St. Louis, Mo.

BONITA
46848

HOLY WOMAN, GRACEFUL GIVER

1 Ho - ly wom - an, grace - ful giv - er,
2 Like the ves - sel, we are bro - ken;
3 In these jars is hid - den trea - sure,
4 Ho - ly wom - an, cost - ly trea - sure,

proph - et, ser - vant, and be - liev - er,
like the oint - ment, we are to - ken
cost - ly fra - grance, Christ - ly plea - sure,
with the jar of al - a - bas - ter,

wom - an with the oint - ment jar,
of God's lov - ing un - to death;
like the Christ, first from the dead,
shows the hid - den gift we are;

rose up near the time ap - point - ed,
like the wom - an, we are serv - ing;
bro - ken for cre - a - tion's whole - ness,
there - fore let us as Christ's ser - vants

broke the seal, Christ's head a - noint - ed
like the scold - ers, ill de - serv - ing
poured out for its com - ing full - ness,
hold our sis - ter in re - mem - brance,

for the com - ing fa - tal hour.
such a rich, for - giv - ing faith.
Proph - et, Ser - vant, Hope and Head.
wom - an with the oint - ment jar.

Text: Susan Palo Cherwien
Music: David Cherwien
Text © 1994 Susan Palo Cherwien, admin. Augsburg Fortress
Music © 1995 Augsburg Fortress

ALABASTER
8 8 7 8 8 7

IN DEEPEST NIGHT

1 In deep-est night, in dark-est days, when harps are hung, no
2 When friend was lost, when love de-ceived, dear Je-sus wept, God
3 When through the wa-ters winds our path, a-round us pain, a-

songs we raise, when si-lence must suf-fice as praise, yet
was be-reaved; so with us in our grief God grieves, and
round us death: deep calls to deep, a sav-ing breath, and

sound-ing in us qui-et-ly there is the song of God.
round a-bout us mourn-ful-ly there are the tears of God.
found be-side us faith-ful-ly there is the love of God.

Text: Susan Palo Cherwien
Music: Emily Maxson Porter
Text © 1995 Susan Palo Cherwien, admin. Augsburg Fortress
Music © 1997 Augsburg Fortress

NICHOLS
8 8 8 8 6

IN SACRED MANNER

1 In sa - cred man - ner may we walk up -
2 In sa - cred man - ner may we see the
3 In sa - cred man - ner may we touch the
4 In sa - cred man - ner may we hear the
5 In sa - cred man - ner may we live a -
6 In sa - cred man - ner may we walk up -

on the fair and lov - ing earth, in beau - ty
lu - mi - nous and lov - ing stars, with won - der
sus - pir - ant and lov - ing green, give hon - or
pound - ing waves, the sear - ing fire, the rush - ing
mong the wise and lov - ing ones, sit hum - bly,
on the fair and lov - ing earth, in beau - ty

move, in beau - ty love the liv - ing round that brought us
and with awe be - hold their ev - er - new cre - a - tive
and give grat - i - tude for shade, for bloom, for gift un -
wind, the sing - ing night, the for - est hymn, the lov - ing
as at sa - ges' feet, by four - legged, finned and feath - ered
move, in beau - ty love the liv - ing round that brought us

birth.   We   stand   on   ho - ly   ground.   We
pow'rs.   The   heav - ens   show   us   God.   The
seen.   The   trees   shall   shout   for   joy.   The
choir.   The   morn - ing   stars   shall   sing.   The
ones.   The   an - i - mals   will   teach.   The
birth.   We   stand   on   ho - ly   ground.   We

1-5

stand   on   ho - ly   ground.
heav - ens   show   us   God.
trees   shall   shout   for   joy.
morn - ing   stars   shall   sing.
an - i - mals   will   teach.

6

stand   on   ho - ly   ground.

Text: Susan Palo Cherwien
Music: Robert Buckley Farlee
Text © 1990 Susan Palo Cherwien, admin. Augsburg Fortress
Music © 1997 Augsburg Fortress

SEATTLE
8 8 8 8 6 6

IN THE DESERT, ON GOD'S MOUNTAIN

1 In the des - ert, on God's moun - tain,
2 On Mount Hor - eb Mo - ses halt - ed,
3 "I AM THAT I AM have called you,"
4 Mo - ses hid his face in ter - ror,
5 La - ter in the wild of Si - nai,
6 Far from des - erts, far from moun - tains,

Mo - ses saw the bush a - flame,
stood un - shod on ho - ly ground,
spoke the in - can - des - cent voice.
of - fered his ob - jec - tions four:
from a - noth - er moun - tain height,
yearns a bound hu - man - i - ty.

won - dered at the fi - 'ry fo - liage,
felt the puls - ing of God's pres - ence,
Mo - ses felt the mes - sage sear - ing
doubt of worth and doubt of tal - ent,
bring - ing prom - ise to his peo - ple,
Filled with fire of ho - ly ground - ing,

heard the crack - ling call his name.
sensed the ho - li - ness a - round.
to the heart of will and choice.
lack of trust and lack of lore.
Mo - ses shone with God's own light.
burn - ing bush - es may we be,

May we no - tice bush - es burn - ing;
May we stop a - mid life's la - bor;
May we pause to ans - wer sum - mons;
May we set a - side ex - cus - es;
May we, not con - sumed, yet burn - ing,
draw - ing all to God's bright pres - ence—

may we won - der at the flame.
may we hon - or ho - ly ground.
may we hear God's burn - ing voice.
may we take the task be - fore.
guide all to the moun - tain height.
bea - cons of di - vin - i - ty.

Text: Susan Palo Cherwien
Music: French folk tune, 17th cent., arr. Ronald A. Nelson
Text © 1989 Susan Palo Cherwien, admin. Augsburg Fortress
Arr. © 1978 *Lutheran Book of Worship*, admin. Augsburg Fortress

PICARDY
8 7 8 7 8 7

IN THE FAIR MORNING

Fear not, O peo-ple! You seek your Je-sus;
Bow not your fac-es, rise up in won - der,

God has act - ed, do not fear.
Christ a - waits you on the way;

Seek him in liv - ing, seek him in lov - ing,
in the fair morn-ing, bright sun a - ris - ing,

but in this grave— he is not here.
Christ waits to greet you to the day.

Text: Susan Palo Cherwien
Music: Mark Sedio
Text © 1995 Susan Palo Cherwien, admin. Augsburg Fortress
Music © 1995 A. M. S. I., Minneapolis, Minn.

FAIR MORNING
5 5 7 5 5 8 D

O BLESSED SPRING

1 O bless- ed spring, where Word and sign em - brace us
2 Through sum - mer heat of youth - ful years, un - cer - tain
3 When au - tumn cools and youth is cold, when limbs their
4 As win - ter comes, as win - ters must, we breathe our
5 Christ, ho - ly Vine, Christ, liv - ing Tree, be praised for

in - to Christ the Vine: here Christ en - joins each one to
faith, re - bel - lious tears, sus - tained by Christ's in - fus - ing
heav - y har - vest hold, then through us, warm, the Christ will
last, re - turn to dust; still held in Christ, our souls take
this blest mys - ter - y: that Word and wa - ter thus re -

be a branch of this life - giv - ing Tree.
rain, the boughs will shout for joy a - gain.
move with gifts of beau - ty, wis - dom, love.
wing and trust the prom - ise of the spring.
vive and join us to your Tree of Life.

Text: Susan Palo Cherwien
Music: Robert Buckley Farlee
Text © 1993 Susan Palo Cherwien, admin. Augsburg Fortress
Music © 1993 Robert Buckley Farlee, Minneapolis, Minn.

BERGLUND
L M

O GRANT US, CHRIST, A DEEP HUMILITY

1 O grant us, Christ, a deep humil - i -
2 O grant us, Christ, a joy - ous char - i -
3 O grant us, Christ, a pure sim - plic - i -
4 Your church, O Christ, with ho - li - ness im -

ty, so that your church a kneel - ing church may be:
ty, so that your church a lov - ing church may be:
ty, so that your church a pray - ing church may be:
bue, so that the church trans - fig - ure in - to you;

kneel - ing in won - der with the shep-herd band,
lov - ing with hands that hold hands nev - er held,
pray - ing with hands that tend and care and bless,
that, drawn in - to your great and mys - tic throng

kneel - ing in beau - ty, oint - ment jar in hand,
lov - ing with tears from deep com - pas - sion welled,
pray - ing with voice a - live with thank - ful - ness,
and fo - cused in one Bod - y and one song,

kneel - ing in dust to write for - giv - en sins,
lov - ing with bread to break, to bless, to share,
pray - ing with eyes that rec - og - nize the Christ,
we see the reign of God come far and broad

kneel - ing in love to wash the feet of friends.
lov - ing with heart of si - lent pain and prayer.
pray - ing with heart a - brim with Par - a - dise.
and kneel be - fore the maj - es - ty of God.

Text: Susan Palo Cherwien
Music: Ronald A. Nelson
Text © 1994 Susan Palo Cherwien, admin. Augsburg Fortress
Music © 1997 Augsburg Fortress

WESTWOOD NEW
10 10 10 10 10 10

O SACRED RIVER

1 O sa-cred Riv - er, from whose flow the stars, the seas, the
2 O sa-cred Dark - ness, from whose night the seed may flow'r, the
3 O sa-cred Beau - ty, from whose Word the o - ceans blast, the
4 O sa-cred Ban - quet, from whose love the thirst- y drink, the

cells were cast, whose play-ful pat - terns brought to life the
spir - it, bloom, whose warm em - brac - es brought to pass cre -
tem - pests play, whose ho - ly pal - ette brought to light the
hun - gry fare, whose in - vi - ta - tion brought to feast the

surg - ing earth, the heav - ens vast: Mur - mur in us, that we
a - tion's fruit, an emp - ty tomb: To your shad - ow us in -
crim - son dawn, trans - lu - cent day: Wake in us the art - ist
im - age lost, the heart's de - spair: To com - pas - sion may we

know that you still with - in us flow.
vite that we may not shun the night.
surd that we man - i - fest your Word.
move that all feast up - on your love.

surd = silent, mute

Text: Susan Palo Cherwien
Music: Mark Sedio
Text © 1988 Susan Palo Cherwien, admin. Augsburg Fortress
Music © 1997 Augsburg Fortress

FLUMEN SACER
888877

RICH IN PROMISE

1 Rich in prom-ise, rich in pres-ent, dry as dust and
2 Run-ning riv-er in the des-ert, wa-ter meets the
3 Par-a-ble of grain and green-ing, par-a-dox of
4 So we move from seed to ripe-ness, so we move from

des-ert sand, bur-ied in the po-tent land,
wil-der-ness, trans-for-ma-tion, more from less,
death and birth, sto-ry of our wait in earth
grain to green, let-ting go of what has been,

deep and dark the grain lies dor - mant:
swol-len seed sends new-ness sky - ward:
for the sac-ra-men-tal rain - ing:
we em-bod-y God's great prom - ise:

Refrain

Be-hold, God does a new thing, through death God brings new life.

Text: Susan Palo Cherwien
Music: Robert Buckley Farlee
Text © 1988 Susan Palo Cherwien, admin. Augsburg Fortress
Music © 1997 Augsburg Fortress

RES NOVA
877876

RISE, O CHURCH, LIKE CHRIST ARISEN

1 Rise, O church, like Christ a - ris - en,
2 Rise, trans - formed, and choose to fol - low
3 Rise, re - mem - ber well the fu - ture
4 Ser - vice be our sure vo - ca - tion;

from this meal of love and grace;
af - ter Christ, though wound - ed, whole;
God has called us to re - ceive;
cour - age be our dai - ly breath;

may we through such love en - vi - sion
bro - ken, shared, our lives are hal - lowed
pres - ent by God's lov - ing nur - ture,
mer - cy be our des - ti - na - tion

whose we are, and whose, our praise.
to re - lease and to con - sole.
spir - it - ed then let us live.
from this day and un - to death.

Al - le - lu - ia, al - le - lu - ia:
Al - le - lu - ia, al - le - lu - ia:
Al - le - lu - ia, al - le - lu - ia:
Al - le - lu - ia, al - le - lu - ia.

God, the won - der of our days.
Christ, our pres - ent, past, and goal.
Spir - it, grace by whom we live.
Rise, O church, a liv - ing faith.

Text: Susan Palo Cherwien
Music: Timothy J. Strand
Text © 1997 Susan Palo Cherwien, admin. Augsburg Fortress
Music © 1997 Augsburg Fortress

SURGE ECCLESIA
878787

SWEET COMING FOR WHICH WE LONG

Sweet com-ing for which we long: soft com-ing of star - voiced Child; still coming in fra - grant meal; swift com-ing for won - drous weal. Sure com-ing, both hope and trial; soon com-ing, our wist - ful song.

Text: Susan Palo Cherwien
Music: Robert Buckley Farlee
Text © 1996 Susan Palo Cherwien, admin. Augsburg Fortress
Music © 1997 Augsburg Fortress

SWEET COMING
7 7 7 7 7 7

TEACH US TO SEEK

1 Teach us to seek on earth the low-est place, to
2 Teach us to mourn with those whom sword has pierced, with
3 Teach us to see in all whom you have made the
4 Teach us to live the un-der-ly-ing One; teach

sit at ta-ble with the hun-gry poor, to beg in noon-tide sun the crust of
them to laugh when cel-e-bra-tion flows; teach us to dance a-round the for-eign
liv-ing im-age of the lov-ing God, and as a host see that all hands are
us to love the oth-er with-out goal; teach us to lose the fear that does not

bread, re-ceive as guest the gift in-to our hand; for
fire, to feel the warmth, to join the cir-cled throng; for
filled be-fore we from the ta-ble take and eat; for
know; teach us to leave the clutch-ing of life's good; for

Love sought out the place of hum - ble birth that
Truth broke bread with peas - ant and with priest to
Wis - dom came and cried dis - par - i - ty that
Peace freed us long hence from fear and hell to

hum - ble kind-ness mark our life on earth. Grant love, O God; grant
change our rend - ing fear in-to a feast. Grant truth, O God; grant
greed may cede to good and char - i - ty. Grant wis - dom, God; grant
stop the rag - ing war up - on our-selves. Grant peace in us; grant

love, O God, that hum - ble kind-ness mark our life on earth.
truth, O God, to change our rend-ing fear in - to a feast.
wis - dom, God, that greed may cede to good and char - i - ty.
peace in us to stop the rag - ing war up - on our - selves.

Text: Susan Palo Cherwien
Music: Robert Buckley Farlee
Text © 1991 Susan Palo Cherwien, admin. Augsburg Fortress
Music © 1997 Augsburg Fortress

PAIDEIA
10 10 10 10 10 10 4 4 10

81

THE JOURNEY WAS CHOSEN

1 The jour-ney was cho-sen when wa-ter was poured, when
2 The jour-ney is strength-ened when, called as a guest, we
3 The jour-ney is ho-ly: to u-nion with Christ, in
4 Come, all, to the wa-ters, you thirst-y, you spare; come,

head was a-noint-ed and priest-hood re-stored; the
share bread and vin-tage, God's roy-al re-past; the
ser-vice and jus-tice and self-sac-ri-fice; the
all, to the ta-ble, en-coun-ter Christ there; come,

jour-ney was cho-sen when, brought to the Lord, we
jour-ney is strength-ened: we rise, fed and blest, as
jour-ney is ho-ly, trans-form-ing and wise for
all, on the jour-ney of cov-e-nant, where all

rose, brought from death in - to
those brought from death in - to
those brought from death in - to
rise, brought from

life.
life.
life.

death in - to life.

Text: Susan Palo Cherwien
Music: Paul Manz
Text © 1995 Susan Palo Cherwien, admin. Augsburg Fortress
Music © 1997 Augsburg Fortress

HIGHLAND PARK
6 5 6 5 6 5 8

1 We sing the one God, whose jour-ney we claim as
2 To emp - ti - ness, void, God's en - er - gy came— a
3 To ex - iles of old, God's mes - sen - ger came— a
4 To faith - ful of old, God's hur - ri - cane came— a
5 O God, the one God, un - name-a - ble Name, who

chil - dren of sto - ry and heirs of the flame: God
burst of i - de - a, a great ball of flame: fused
pil - lar of cloud and a col - umn of flame, to
roar - ing, a ting - ling, and bright tongues of flame that
formed us in wis - dom and sparked us to flame, we

mold - ed us, mar - ried us, called us to come, and
beau - ty and or - der and fired us of clay. Cre -
lead them to prom - ise, a cov - e - nant's dawn. And
filled them with pas - sion, the Spir - it of God. And
join in pro - ces - sion a - cross time and space and

set in us yearn-ing to find our way home. We
a - tion cre - a - tor cre - ates yet to - day: the
now in this peo - ple, the jour - ney goes on: hand
now in that Spir - it, the church burns a - broad: so
share in your sto - ry in this age and place. All

jour - ney in sto - ry, pro - found as the sea, de -
can - yons, the crea - tures, the day - light, the dark, all
vis - i - ble clasp-ing in - vis - i - ble hand, as
loved in - to be - ing, the church then a - vows a
praise be to you, for you call us to come: our

scen - dants and friends of a great com - pa - ny:
spi - ral - ing out from the same ho - ly spark.
count - less as stars and un - num - bered as sand. .
life lived a - fire as Christ's pas - sion - ate Spouse.
Mak - er, De - liv - er - er, Lov - er, and Home.

Text: Susan Palo Cherwien
Music: David Cherwien
Text © 1988 Susan Palo Cherwien, admin. Augsburg Fortress
Music © 1997 Augsburg Fortress

JOURNEY HOME
10 11 11 11 11 11

HYMNS WITH
MELODIES

A RAM'S HORN BLASTING BARREN HILLS

1 A ram's horn blast-ing bar-ren hills, the
2 In praise the voic-es vi-brant rise as
3 En-heart-ened by the Spir-it-song, and
4 Great God, who gave us mys-ter-y, who

bells which sleep-ing cit-y prod, call
one, the great en-light-ened crowd— di -
healed, like Saul, by god-ly guest, we
clothed the stars in song di-vine, be

wor-ship to the wak-ing world:
ver-si-ty in u-ni-son,
sing, we soar, we rise to live,
pres-ent in our har-mo-ny—

Laud your God.
clothed in cloud.
bless-ing blest.
sign in sine.

Text: Susan Palo Cherwien
Music: Janet Hill
Text © 1987 Susan Palo Cherwien, admin. Augsburg Fortress
Music © 1997 Augsburg Fortress

SIGN IN SINE
8 8 8 3

AS THE DARK AWAITS THE DAWN

1 As the dark a - waits the dawn,
2 As the blue ex - pec - tant hour
3 As the moon re - flects the sun
4 Shine your fu - ture on this place,

so we a - wait your light. O Star of
be - fore the sil - v'ring skies, we long to
un - til the night's de - crease, may we your
en - light - en ev - 'ry guest, that through us

prom - ise, scat - ter night, lov - ing bright, lov - ing
see your day a - rise, whole and wise, whole and
heal - ing light re - lease, liv - ing peace, liv - ing
stream your ho - li - ness, bright and blest, bright and

bright, till shades of fear are gone.
wise, O lu - cent Morn - ing Star.
peace, un - to your ho - ly dawn.
blest; come dawn, O Sun of grace.

Text: Susan Palo Cherwien
Music: Carl Schalk
Text © 1996 Susan Palo Cherwien, admin. Augsburg Fortress
Music © 1997 Augsburg Fortress

LUCENT
7 6 8 6 6

BELOVED, GOD'S CHOSEN

1 Be - lov - ed, God's cho - sen, put
2 With - in, call forth Wis - dom, to
3 Be - lov - ed, God's cho - sen, put

on as a gar - ment com - pas - sion, for - give - ness, and
dwell in you rich - ly; let peace rule your hearts and that
on as a gar - ment com - pas - sion, for - give - ness, and

good - ness of heart. A - bove all, be - fore all, let love be your
peace be of Christ. And from the heart's cham - ber, be - lov - ed and
good - ness of heart. A - bove all, be - fore all, let love be your

rai - ment that binds in - to one ev - 'ry dis - so - nant part.
ho - ly, let sing - ing thanks - giv - ing to God ev - er rise.
rai - ment that binds in - to one ev - 'ry dis - so - nant part.

Text: Susan Palo Cherwien
Music: Robert A. Hobby
Text © 1994 Susan Palo Cherwien, admin. Augsburg Fortress
Music © 1997 Augsburg Fortress

ANDREW'S SONG
6 6 11 D

BLESSING BE AND GLORY

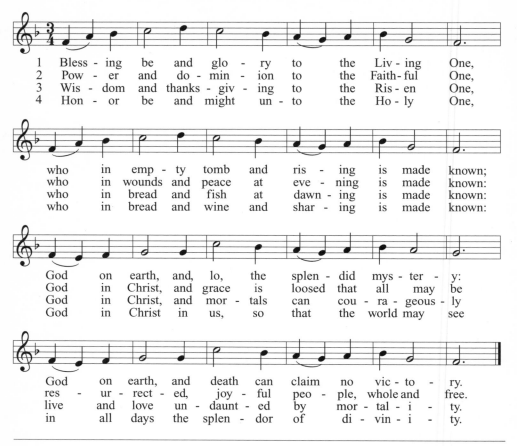

1 Bless - ing be and glo - ry to the Liv - ing One,
2 Pow - er and do - min - ion to the Faith- ful One,
3 Wis - dom and thanks - giv - ing to the Ris - en One,
4 Hon - or be and might un - to the Ho - ly One,

who in emp - ty tomb and ris - ing is made known;
who in wounds and peace at eve - ning is made known:
who in bread and fish at dawn - ing is made known:
who in bread and wine and shar - ing is made known:

God on earth, and, lo, the splen - did mys - ter - y:
God in Christ, and grace is loosed that all may be
God in Christ, and mor - tals can cou - ra - geous - ly
God in Christ in us, so that the world may see

God on earth, and death can claim no vic - to - ry.
res - ur - rect - ed, joy - ful peo - ple, whole and free.
live and love un - daunt - ed by mor - tal - i - ty.
in all days the splen - dor of di - vin - i - ty.

Text: Susan Palo Cherwien
Music: French carol
Text © 1995 Susan Palo Cherwien, admin. Augsburg Fortress

NOUS ALLONS
11 11 11 11

CHRIST, BURNING WISDOM

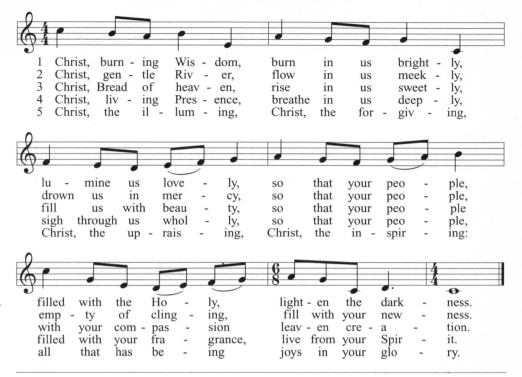

1 Christ, burn - ing Wis - dom, burn in us bright - ly,
2 Christ, gen - tle Riv - er, flow in us meek - ly,
3 Christ, Bread of heav - en, rise in us sweet - ly,
4 Christ, liv - ing Pres - ence, breathe in us deep - ly,
5 Christ, the il - lum - ing, Christ, the for - giv - ing,

lu - mine us love - ly, so that your peo - ple,
drown us in mer - cy, so that your peo - ple,
fill us with beau - ty, so that your peo - ple
sigh through us whol - ly, so that your peo - ple,
Christ, the up - rais - ing, Christ, the in - spir - ing:

filled with the Ho - ly, light - en the dark - ness.
emp - ty of cling - ing, fill with your new - ness.
with your com - pas - sion leav - en cre - a - tion.
filled with your fra - grance, live from your Spir - it.
all that has be - ing joys in your glo - ry.

Text: Susan Palo Cherwien
Music: Janet Hill
Text © 1994 Susan Palo Cherwien, admin. Augsburg Fortress
Music © 1997 Augsburg Fortress

TAUNTON GAP
5 5 5 5 5 5

CHRIST IS THE LIFE

1 Christ is the life of all that is, God's pure cre - a - tive Word,
2 Christ is the death of all that is, a broad and beck - 'ning tomb,
3 Christ is the death of all that is, a bright, con - sum - ing fire,
4 Christ is the life of all that is, Be - gin - ning and the End;

whose pow'r be - yond and through all space the worlds to Be - ing stirred.
who wel - comes us from well - worn ways to dark - ness of the womb.
whose flames re - quire our pri - or self as kin - dling for the pyre.
cre - a - tive force, most peace - ful death, trans - form - ing burn - ing brand.

Christ is the life be - yond all time, cre - a - tion's birth and breath,
Christ is the death, the sink - ing down past all de - sire and fear,
Christ is the death of dust - y days of un - cre - a - tive strife,
Christ is the life, in whose wise love cre - a - tion lives and dies

whose la - bor brings all things to be and brings all things to death.
whose prom - ise in the gen - tle dark bids new - ness to ap - pear.
for out from fire we tread up - on the thresh - old of new life.
and thus for - ev - er - more shall bless the Source, the liv - ing Christ.

Text: Susan Palo Cherwien
Music: English melody
Text © 1989 Susan Palo Cherwien, admin. Augsburg Fortress

KINGSFOLD
C M D

CREATOR GOD, WHO GAVE US LIFE

1 Cre - a - tor God, who gave us life, who
2 In - fuse us with your fer - tile grace and
3 That through your art - ists, thus in - spired, all

breathed us in - to song, who set in us cre -
con - se - crate our art; bring spring - time to our
bar - ren - ness may flee; all hearts and minds be

a - tive drive, from whom our ut - most dreams de - rive, to
wil - der - ness where void and tal - ent in - ter - face and
o - pened wide and minds thus o - pened glimpse in - side your

whom all arts be - long, to whom all arts be - long:
pow'r to us im - part, and pow'r to us im - part;
love and maj - es - ty, your love and maj - es - ty.

Text: Susan Palo Cherwien
Music: C. Hubert H. Parry
Text © 1987 Susan Palo Cherwien, admin. Augsburg Fortress

REPTON
8 6 8 8 6

DAY OF ARISING

1 Day of a - ris - ing, Christ on the road - way,
2 When we are walk - ing, doubt - ful and dread - ing,
3 Lo, I am with you, Je - sus has spo - ken.
4 Christ, our com - pan - ion, hope for the jour - ney,

un - known com - pan - ion walks with his own.
blind - ed by sad - ness, slow - ness of heart,
This is Christ's prom - ise, this is Christ's sign:
bread of com - pas - sion, o - pen our eyes.

When they in - vite him, as fades the first day,
yet Christ walks with us ev - er a - wait - ing
when the church gath - ers, when bread is bro - ken,
Grant us your vi - sion, set all hearts burn - ing

and bread is bro - ken, Christ is made known.
our in - vi - ta - tion: Stay, do not part.
there Christ is with us in bread and wine.
that all cre - a - tion with you may rise.

Text: Susan Palo Cherwien
Music: Gaelic melody
Text © 1996 Susan Palo Cherwien, admin. Augsburg Fortress

BUNESSAN
5 5 5 4 D

FROM LOVING HANDS

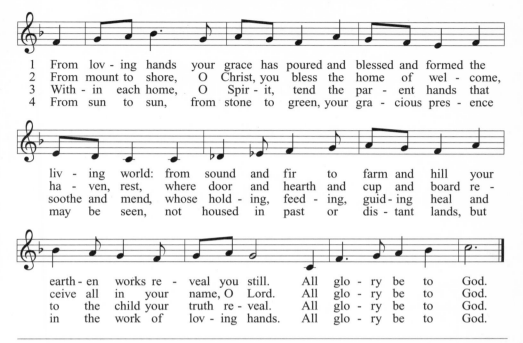

1 From lov - ing hands your grace has poured and blessed and formed the
2 From mount to shore, O Christ, you bless the home of wel - come,
3 With - in each home, O Spir - it, tend the par - ent hands that
4 From sun to sun, from stone to green, your gra - cious pres - ence

liv - ing world: from sound and fir to farm and hill your
ha - ven, rest, where door and hearth and cup and board re -
soothe and mend, whose hold - ing, feed - ing, guid - ing heal and
may be seen, not housed in past or dis - tant lands, but

earth - en works re - veal you still. All glo - ry be to God.
ceive all in your name, O Lord. All glo - ry be to God.
to the child your truth re - veal. All glo - ry be to God.
in the work of lov - ing hands. All glo - ry be to God.

Text: Susan Palo Cherwien
Music: David Cherwien
Text © 1997 Susan Palo Cherwien, admin. Augsburg Fortress
Music © 1997 Augsburg Fortress

TORVEND
8 8 8 8 6

GLORY TO YOU, GOD

1 Glo - ry to you, God, for yours is the earth;
2 Glo - ry to you, God, for yours is the earth;
3 Glo - ry to you, God, for yours is the earth;

yours is the prom - ise, the bless - ing, the birth.
yours the ho - san - nas, the dy - ing, re - birth.
yours the a - noint - ing, the ra - di - ant worth.

Ours the re - joic - ing for Word giv - en frame;
Ours the re - joic - ing for na - ture re - claimed;
Ours the re - joic - ing for spir - its a - flame;

ours the thanks - giv - ing to your ho - ly name.

Ours be the tell - ing of deeds great - ly done;

yours be the glo - ry, O God, yours a - lone.

Text: Susan Palo Cherwien
Music: J. Bert Carlson
© 1995 Augsburg Fortress

YOURS ALONE
10 10 10 10 10 10

GOD HAS CALLED US

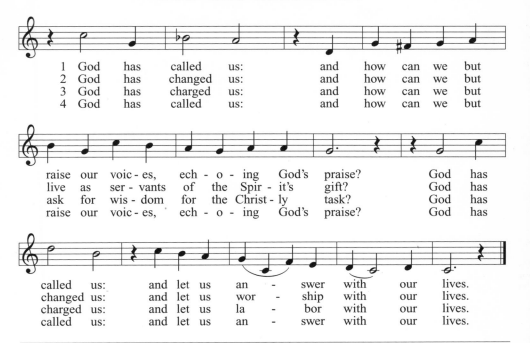

1 God has called us: and how can we but
2 God has changed us: and how can we but
3 God has charged us: and how can we but
4 God has called us: and how can we but

raise our voic-es, ech-o-ing God's praise? God has
live as ser-vants of the Spir-it's gift? God has
ask for wis-dom for the Christ-ly task? God has
raise our voic-es, ech-o-ing God's praise? God has

called us: and let us an - swer with our lives.
changed us: and let us wor - ship with our lives.
charged us: and let us la - bor with our lives.
called us: and let us an - swer with our lives.

Text: Susan Palo Cherwien
Music: David Cherwien
Text © 1994 Susan Palo Cherwien, admin. Augsburg Fortress
Music © 1996 Concordia Publishing House, St. Louis, Mo.

BONITA
4 6 8 4 8

HOLY WOMAN, GRACEFUL GIVER

1 Ho - ly wom - an, grace - ful giv - er,
2 Like the ves - sel, we are bro - ken;
3 In these jars is hid - den trea - sure,
4 Ho - ly wom - an, cost - ly trea - sure,

proph - et, ser - vant, and be - liev - er,
like the oint - ment, we are to - ken
cost - ly fra - grance, Christ - ly plea - sure,
with the jar of al - a - bas - ter,

wom - an with the oint - ment jar,
of God's lov - ing un - to death;
like the Christ, first from the dead,
shows the hid - den gift we are;

rose up near the time ap - point - ed,
like the wom - an, we are serv - ing;
bro - ken for cre - a - tion's whole - ness,
there - fore let us as Christ's ser - vants

broke the seal, Christ's head a - noint - ed
like the scold - ers, ill de - serv - ing
poured out for its com - ing full - ness,
hold our sis - ter in re - mem - brance,

for the com - ing fa - tal hour.
such a rich, for - giv - ing faith.
Proph - et, Ser - vant, Hope and Head.
wom - an with the oint - ment jar.

Text: Susan Palo Cherwien
Music: David Cherwien
Text © 1994 Susan Palo Cherwien, admin. Augsburg Fortress
Music © 1995 Augsburg Fortress

ALABASTER
8 8 7 8 8 7

IN DEEPEST NIGHT

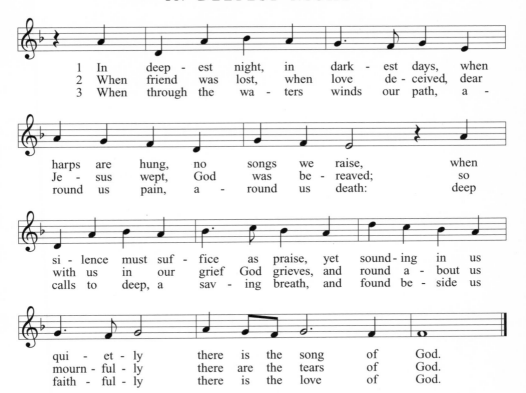

1 In deep - est night, in dark - est days, when
2 When friend was lost, when love de - ceived, dear
3 When through the wa - ters winds our path, a -

harps are hung, no songs we raise, when
Je - sus wept, God was be - reaved; so
round us pain, a - round us death: deep

si - lence must suf - fice as praise, yet sound - ing in us
with us in our grief God grieves, and round a - bout us
calls to deep, a sav - ing breath, and found be - side us

qui - et - ly there is the song of God.
mourn - ful - ly there are the tears of God.
faith - ful - ly there is the love of God.

Text: Susan Palo Cherwien
Music: Emily Maxson Porter
Text © 1995 Susan Palo Cherwien, admin. Augsburg Fortress
Music © 1997 Augsburg Fortress

NICHOLS
8 8 8 8 6

IN SACRED MANNER

1 In sa - cred man - ner may we walk up-
2 In sa - cred man - ner may we see the
3 In sa - cred man - ner may we touch the
4 In sa - cred man - ner may we hear the
5 In sa - cred man - ner may we live a-
6 In sa - cred man - ner may we walk up-

on the fair and lov - ing earth, in beau - ty move, in
lu - mi - nous and lov - ing stars, with won - der and with
sus - pir - ant and lov - ing green, give hon - or and give
pound- ing waves, the sear - ing fire, the rush - ing wind, the
mong the wise and lov - ing ones, sit hum - bly, as at
on the fair and lov - ing earth, in beau - ty move, in

beau - ty love the liv - ing round that brought us birth. We
awe be - hold their ev - er - new cre - a - tive pow'rs. The
grat - i - tude for shade, for bloom, for gift un - seen. The
sing - ing night, the for - est hymn, the lov - ing choir. The
sa - ges' feet, by four - legged, finned and feath - ered ones. The
beau - ty love the liv - ing round that brought us birth. We

stand on ho - ly ground. We stand on ho - ly ground.
heav - ens show us God. The heav - ens show us God.
trees shall shout for joy. The trees shall shout for joy.
morn - ing stars shall sing. The morn - ing stars shall sing.
an - i - mals will teach. The an - i - mals will teach.
stand on ho - ly ground. We stand on ho - ly ground.

Text: Susan Palo Cherwien
Music: Robert Buckley Farlee
Text © 1990 Susan Palo Cherwien, admin. Augsburg Fortress
Music © 1997 Augsburg Fortress

SEATTLE
888866

IN THE DESERT, ON GOD'S MOUNTAIN

1 In the des - ert, on God's moun - tain, Mo - ses saw the
2 On Mount Ho - reb Mo - ses halt - ed, stood un - shod on
3 "I AM THAT I AM have called you," spoke the in - can -
4 Mo - ses hid his face in ter - ror, of - fered his ob -
5 Lat - er in the wild of Si - nai, from an - oth - er
6 Far from des - erts, far from moun - tains, yearns a bound hu -

bush a - flame, won - dered at the fi - 'ry
ho - ly ground, felt the puls - ing of God's
des - cent voice. Mo - ses felt the mes - sage
jec - tions four: doubt of worth and doubt of
moun - tain height, bring - ing prom - ise to his
man - i - ty. Filled with fire of ho - ly

fo - liage, heard the crack - ling call his name.
pres - ence, sensed the ho - li - ness a - round.
sear - ing to the heart of will and choice.
tal - ent, lack of trust and lack of lore.
peo - ple, Mo - ses shone with God's own light.
ground - ing, burn - ing bush - es may we be,

May we no - tice bush - es burn - ing;
May we stop a - mid life's la - bor;
May we pause to an - swer sum - mons;
May we set a - side ex - cus - es;
May we, not con - sumed, yet burn - ing,
draw - ing all to God's bright pres - ence—

may we won - der at the flame.
may we hon - or ho - ly ground.
may we hear God's burn - ing voice.
may we take the task be - fore.
guide all to the moun - tain height.
bea - cons of di - vin - i - ty.

Text: Susan Palo Cherwien
Music: French folk tune, 17th cent.
Text © 1989 Susan Palo Cherwien, admin. Augsburg Fortress

PICARDY
8 7 8 7 8 7

IN THE FAIR MORNING

1 In the fair morn-ing, soft sun a-ris - ing,
2 Why stand there weep-ing? Why weep in sor - row?

bring - ing spice, ex - pect - ing death,
Je - sus lives, and fear has fled.

we seek the bod - y, sad - ness and si - lence,
Roll a - way sad - ness, view this a - ris - ing:

and hear an an - gel voice in - stead:
Je - sus is raised, and death is dead.

Fear not, O peo - ple! You seek your Je - sus;
Bow not your fac - es, rise up in won - der,

God has act - ed, do not fear.
Christ a - waits you on the way;

Seek him in liv - ing, seek him in lov - ing,
in the fair morn - ing, bright sun a - ris - ing,

but in this grave— he is not here.
Christ waits to greet you to the day.

Text: Susan Palo Cherwien
Music: Mark Sedio
Text © 1995 Susan Palo Cherwien, admin. Augsburg Fortress
Music © 1995 A. M. S. I., Minneapolis, MN

FAIR MORNING
5 5 7 5 5 8 D

O BLESSED SPRING

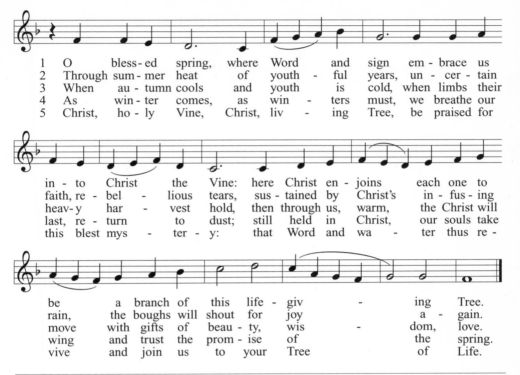

1 O bless-ed spring, where Word and sign em-brace us
2 Through sum-mer heat of youth-ful years, un-cer-tain
3 When au-tumn cools and youth is cold, when limbs their
4 As win-ter comes, as win-ters must, we breathe our
5 Christ, ho-ly Vine, Christ, liv-ing Tree, be praised for

in-to Christ the Vine: here Christ en-joins each one to
faith, re-bel-lious tears, sus-tained by Christ's in-fus-ing
heav-y har-vest hold, then through us, warm, the Christ will
last, re-turn to dust; still held in Christ, our souls take
this blest mys-ter-y: that Word and wa-ter thus re-

be a branch of this life-giv-ing Tree.
rain, the boughs will shout for joy a-gain.
move with gifts of beau-ty, wis-dom, love.
wing and trust the prom-ise of the spring.
vive and join us to your Tree of Life.

Text: Susan Palo Cherwien
Music: Robert Buckley Farlee
Text © 1993 Susan Palo Cherwien, admin. Augsburg Fortress
Music © 1993 Robert Buckley Farlee, Minneapolis, Minn.

BERGLUND
L M

O GRANT US, CHRIST, A DEEP HUMILITY

1 O grant us, Christ, a deep humil - i -
2 O grant us, Christ, a joy - ous char - i -
3 O grant us, Christ, a pure sim - plic - i -
4 Your church, O Christ, with ho - li - ness im -

ty, so that your church a kneel - ing church may be:
ty, so that your church a lov - ing church may be:
ty, so that your church a pray - ing church may be:
bue, so that the church trans - fig - ure in - to you;

kneel - ing in won - der with the shep-herd band,
lov - ing with hands that hold hands nev - er held,
pray - ing with hands that tend and care and bless,
that, drawn in - to your great and mys - tic throng

kneel - ing in beau - ty, oint - ment jar in hand,
lov - ing with tears from deep com - pas - sion welled,
pray - ing with voice a - live with thank - ful - ness,
and fo - cused in one Bod - y and one song,

kneel - ing in dust to write for - giv - en sins,
lov - ing with bread to break, to bless, to share,
pray - ing with eyes that rec - og - nize the Christ,
we see the reign of God come far and broad

kneel - ing in love to wash the feet of friends.
lov - ing with heart of si - lent pain and prayer.
pray - ing with heart a - brim with Par - a - dise.
and kneel be - fore the maj - es - ty of God.

Text: Susan Palo Cherwien
Music: Ronald A. Nelson
Text © 1994 Susan Palo Cherwien, admin. Augsburg Fortress
Music © 1997 Augsburg Fortress

WESTWOOD NEW
10 10 10 10 10 10

O SACRED RIVER

1 O sa - cred Riv - er, from whose flow the
2 O sa - cred Dark - ness, from whose night the
3 O sa - cred Beau - ty, from whose Word the
4 O sa - cred Ban - quet, from whose love the

stars, the seas, the cells were cast, whose play - ful
seed may flow'r, the spir - it, bloom, whose warm em -
o - ceans blast, the tem - pests play, whose ho - ly
thirst - y drink, the hun - gry fare, whose in - vi -

pat - terns brought to life the surg - ing earth, the
brac - es brought to pass cre - a - tion's fruit, an
pal - ette brought to light the crim - son dawn, trans -
ta - tion brought to feast the im - age lost, the

heav - ens vast: Mur - mur in us, that we
emp - ty tomb: To your shad - ow us in -
lu - cent day: Wake in us the ar - tist
heart's de - spair: To com - pas - sion may we

know that you still with - in us flow.
vite that we may not shun the night.
surd that we man - i - fest your Word.
move that all feast up - on your love.

surd = silent, mute

Text: Susan Palo Cherwien
Music: Mark Sedio
Text © 1988 Susan Palo Cherwien, admin. Augsburg Fortress
Music © 1997 Augsburg Fortress

FLUMEN SACER
8 8 8 8 7 7

RICH IN PROMISE

1 Rich in prom - ise, rich in pres - ent,
2 Run - ning riv - er in the des - ert,
3 Par - a - ble of grain and green - ing,
4 So we move from seed to ripe - ness,

dry as dust and des - ert sand,
wa - ter meets the wil - der - ness,
par - a - dox of death and birth,
so we move from grain to green,

bur - ied in the po - tent land,
trans - for - ma - tion, more from less,
sto - ry of our wait in earth
let - ting go of what has been,

deep and dark the grain lies dor - mant:
swol - len seed sends new - ness sky - ward:
for the sac - ra - men - tal rain - ing:
we em - bod - y God's great prom - ise:

Refrain

Be - hold, God does a new thing, through death God brings new life.

Text: Susan Palo Cherwien
Music: Robert Buckley Farlee
Text © 1988 Susan Palo Cherwien, admin. Augsburg Fortress
Music © 1997 Augsburg Fortress

RES NOVA
8 7 7 8 7 6

RISE, O CHURCH, LIKE CHRIST ARISEN

1 Rise, O church, like Christ a - ris - en,
2 Rise, trans - formed, and choose to fol - low
3 Rise, re - mem - ber well the fu - ture
4 Ser - vice be our sure vo - ca - tion;

from this meal of love and grace;
af - ter Christ, though wound - ed, whole;
God has called us to re - ceive;
cour - age be our dai - ly breath;

may we through such love en - vi - sion
bro - ken, shared, our lives are hal - lowed
pres - ent by God's lov - ing nur - ture,
mer - cy be our des - ti - na - tion

whose we are, and whose, our praise.
to re - lease and to con - sole.
spir - it - ed then let us live.
from this day and un - to death.

Al - le - lu - ia, al - le - lu - ia;
Al - le - lu - ia, al - le - lu - ia;
Al - le - lu - ia, al - le - lu - ia;
Al - le - lu - ia, al - le - lu - ia.

God, the won - der of our days.
Christ, our pres - ent, past, and goal.
Spir - it, grace by whom we live.
Rise, O church, a liv - ing faith.

Text: Susan Palo Cherwien
Music: Timothy J. Strand
Text © 1997 Susan Palo Cherwien, admin. Augsburg Fortress
Music © 1997 Augsburg Fortress

SURGE ECCLESIA
8 7 8 7 8 7

SWEET COMING FOR WHICH WE LONG

Sweet com-ing for which we long: soft com-ing of star-voiced
Child; still com-ing in fra-grant meal; swift
com-ing for won-drous weal. Sure com-ing, both hope and
trial; soon com-ing, our wist-ful song.

Text: Susan Palo Cherwien
Music: Robert Buckley Farlee
Text © 1996 Susan Palo Cherwien, admin. Augsburg Fortress
Music © 1997 Augsburg Fortress

SWEET COMING
7 7 7 7 7 7

TEACH US TO SEEK

1 Teach us to seek on earth the low - est place, to
2 Teach us to mourn with those whom sword has pierced, with
3 Teach us to see in all whom you have made the
4 Teach us to live the un - der - ly - ing One; teach

sit at ta - ble with the hun- gry poor, to beg in noon-tide sun the crust of
them to laugh when cel - e - bra- tion flows; teach us to dance a-round the for-eign
liv - ing im - age of the lov-ing God, and as a host see that all hands are
us to love the oth - er with-out goal; teach us to lose the fear that does not

bread, re - ceive as guest the gift in - to our hand; for
fire, to feel the warmth, to join the cir - cled throng; for
filled be - fore we from the ta - ble take and eat; for
know; teach us to leave the clutch-ing of life's good; for

Love sought out the place of hum - ble birth that
Truth broke bread with peas - ant and with priest to
Wis - dom came and cried dis - par - i - ty that
Peace freed us long hence from fear and hell to

hum - ble kind-ness mark our life on earth. Grant love, O God; grant
change our rend - ing fear in - to a feast. Grant truth, O God; grant
greed may cede to good and char-i - ty. Grant wis - dom, God; grant
stop the rag - ing war up - on our-selves. Grant peace in us; grant

love, O God, that hum - ble kind-ness mark our life on earth.
truth, O God, to change our rend-ing fear in - to a feast.
wis - dom, God, that greed may cede to good and char-i - ty.
peace in us to stop the rag - ing war up - on our - selves.

Text: Susan Palo Cherwien
Music: Robert Buckley Farlee
Text © 1991 Susan Palo Cherwien, admin. Augsburg Fortress
Music © 1997 Augsburg Fortress

PAIDEIA
10 10 10 10 10 10 4 4 10

THE JOURNEY WAS CHOSEN

1 The jour-ney was cho-sen when wa-ter was poured, when
2 The jour-ney is strength-ened when, called as a guest, we
3 The jour-ney is ho-ly: to u-nion with Christ, in
4 Come, all, to the wa-ters, you thirst-y, you spare; come,

head was a-noint-ed and priest-hood re-stored; the
share bread and vin-tage, God's roy-al re-past; the
ser-vice and jus-tice and self-sac-ri-fice; the
all, to the ta-ble, en-coun-ter Christ there; come,

jour-ney was cho-sen when, brought to the Lord, we
jour-ney is strength-ened: we rise, fed and blest, as
jour-ney is ho-ly, trans-form-ing and wise for
all, on the jour-ney of cov-e-nant, where all

rose, brought from death in-to life.
those brought from death in-to life.
those brought from death in-to life.
rise, brought from death in-to life.

Text: Susan Palo Cherwien
Music: Paul Manz
Text © 1995 Susan Palo Cherwien, admin. Augsburg Fortress
Music © 1997 Augsburg Fortress

HIGHLAND PARK
6 5 6 5 6 5 8

WE SING THE ONE GOD

1 We sing the one God, whose jour-ney we claim as
2 To emp-ti-ness, void, God's en-er-gy came— a
3 To ex-iles of old, God's mes-sen-ger came— a
4 To faith-ful of old, God's hur-ri-cane came— a
5 O God, the one God, un-name-a-ble Name, who

chil-dren of sto-ry and heirs of the flame: God
burst of i-de-a, a great ball of flame: fused
pil-lar of cloud and a col-umn of flame, to
roar-ing, a ting-ling, and bright tongues of flame that
formed us in wis-dom and sparked us to flame, we

mold-ed us, mar-ried us, called us to come, and
beau-ty and or-der and fired us of clay. Cre -
lead them to prom-ise, a cov-e-nant's dawn. And
filled them with pas-sion, the Spir-it of God. And
join in pro-ces-sion a-cross time and space and

set in us yearn-ing to find our way home. We
a-tion cre-a-tor cre-ates yet to-day: the
now in this peo-ple, the jour-ney goes on: hand
now in that Spir-it, the church burns a-broad: so
share in your sto-ry in this age and place. All

jour-ney in sto-ry, pro-found as the sea, de -
can-yons, the crea-tures, the day-light, the dark, all
vis-i-ble clasp-ing in-vis-i-ble hand, as
loved in-to be-ing, the church then a-vows a
praise be to you, for you call us to come: our

scen-dants and friends of a great com-pa-ny:
spi-ral-ing out from the same ho-ly spark.
count-less as stars and un-num-bered as sand.
life lived a-fire as Christ's pas-sion-ate Spouse.
Mak-er, De-liv-er-er, Lov-er, and Home.

Text: Susan Palo Cherwien
Music: David Cherwien
Text © 1988 Susan Palo Cherwien, admin. Augsburg Fortress
Music © 1997 Augsburg Fortress

JOURNEY HOME
10 11 11 11 11 11

APPENDIXES

NOTES ON THE HYMNS

A ram's horn blasting barren hills
   Drawing upon Martin Luther's words in the Small Catechism:
   "[the Holy Ghost] calls, gathers, enlightens, and sanctifies the
   whole Christian church on earth" (Third Article, Apostles' Creed),
   this reflection on worship and music as servants of the Divine uses
   images from 2 Chron. 5:12-13, Gen. 12:2, 1 Sam. 16:15,16 and Job
   38:7. The sine wave is the essential shape of sung sound.

As the dark awaits the dawn
   An Advent hymn written for composer John Helgen, Minneapolis,
   who asked for a text that reflected the broad meanings of the season. Images are drawn from Num. 24:17, 2 Peter 1:19, Rev. 22:16,
   Heb. 1:3, and Mal. 4:2.

Beloved, God's chosen
   A versification of Colossians 3:12-16 commissioned by First
   Lutheran Church, Freeport, Illinois to honor Twila K. Schock on
   the occasion of the rededication of the church's pipe organ.

Blessing be and glory
   An evocation of the resurrection appearances of Jesus Christ as
   recorded in John 20:19-31, John 21:9-14 and Luke 24:28-35,
   framed in the hymnic language of Rev. 7:12.

Bright joining (Meditations on the Cross)
   A meditation on how the coming together of the equal arms of
   the cross reflects the incarnation and crucifixion of Christ, shapes
   our baptismal life, and signals the transformation of the universe.

Christ, burning Wisdom
   A hymn to the Christ in whom "all things hold together" (Col.
   1:15-20), as represented by fire, water, earth (bread), and air.

Christ is the life

"If we die with the Lord, we will live with the Lord." (Rom. 14:8)
"Buried in a death like his, we too shall rise." (Rom. 6:3–9)
"When Christ calls a man, he bids him come and die." (Dietrich Bonhoeffer)

Creator God, who gave us life

This hymn was composed in the three-part form of a collect prayer, roughly based on the prayer for church musicians and artists in *Lutheran Book of Worship*.

Day of arising

Based on Luke 24:13–35, the meeting with the risen Christ on the Emmaus road, this hymn was commissioned for the 1996 annual assembly of the Minneapolis Area Synod of the Evangelical Lutheran Church in America.

From loving hands

Samuel Torvend commissioned this text for the fiftieth wedding anniversary of his parents, Silas and Alice Torvend, and suggested its flow of thought and imagery: a hymn of thanksgiving to God for the creation, for the home of welcome, for the loving hands of parents.

Glory to you, God

Commissioned for the Lutheran worship supplement *With One Voice* as an offertory hymn in the Service of Word and Prayer, this text contains stanzas for each of the three major divisions of the church year (the incarnation cycle, the paschal cycle, the season after Pentecost).

God has called us

First Lutheran Church, Lincoln, Nebraska commissioned this hymn for its 125th anniversary, which had "living the legacy of faith" as its theme.

Holy woman, graceful giver

Written for the 25th anniversary of the ordination of women in the ELCA and its predecessors, the hymn is based on the account of the woman with the jar of ointment (Mark 14:3-9). It celebrates the hidden treasures in all God's people—female and male, clergy and lay—with Christ at their center.

In deepest night

This text came into being in 1995 after a class on "God and Human Suffering" taught by Terence Fretheim, and in response to William Raabe's commissioning of a text on Christian grief. It is dedicated in memory of Van Nichols of Minneapolis, whose death occurred at about the same time. Images are from Isa. 43:1-2, Isa. 53:3-4, Isa. 42:3, John 11:35, Isa. 16:9, Mark 14:34, Ps. 65:2, Ps. 30:5, Ps. 137, Ps. 42:7–8.

In sacred manner

This hymn on creation was written in response to the class "Fate of the Earth" taught by Bill Hill, philosophy, and Tony Gramza, biology, at Mundelein College, Chicago. Each stanza begins with the native American prayer that we may walk "in a sacred manner upon earth," and closes with a biblical image (Exod. 3:5; Ps. 19:1; Ps. 96:12; Job 12:7).

In the desert, on God's mountain

An experiment in a 16th century German technique of versifying a biblical story and then offering a possible application resulted in this hymn on the burning bush story from Exodus 3:1-8b, 10-15 (appointed for the Third Sunday in Lent, year C, in the Revised Common Lectionary).

In the fair morning

Based on Matthew 28:1-10 and Luke 24:1-7, this text is a *lectio divina* meditation on the resurrection morning.

O blessed spring

Above the baptismal font at Lutheran Church of the Good
Shepherd, Minneapolis, hangs a bronze sculpture by Paul Granlund
entitled LIFE-TREE. This hymn was shaped by the seasons of life
portrayed in the sculpture and was written for the baptismal life of
Good Shepherd parish. It is based on the scripture verse Granlund
chose: "I am the vine, you are the branches" (John 15:5).

O grant us, Christ, a deep humility

This prayer for a servant church was commissioned by Westwood
Lutheran Church, St. Louis Park, Minnesota for its 50th anniversary. "Let the same mind be in you that was in Jesus Christ, who,
though he was in the form of God, did not regard equality with
God as something to be exploited, but emptied himself, taking the
form of a slave. . ." (Phil. 2:5-7).

O sacred River

The sermons of Meister Eckhart (1260-1329) influenced these
meditations on God and the spiritual journey. Images are drawn
from Ps. 1:3, Ps. 46:4 (River); Gen. 15:12, Deut. 5:22-23
(Darkness); Ps. 27:4, Ps. 96:6 (Beauty); Luke 14:12, 24, Matt. 22,
Luke 14:13, Isa. 25:6 (Banquet).

O Sea, mystic Source

Written in haiku because of its three line form, "O Sea" is an
exploration into non-anthropocentric images of the Trinity. It is in
four verses rather than three, because the totality of God surpasses
even our finest concepts. Its images are from Eccl. 1:7, Rev. 22:1-4,
and Isa. 55:10.

Rich in promise

Along with "In the desert", this text was written for Lenten peri-
copes which often are "hymnless," in this case the Fifth Sunday in
Lent (years B and C): Isa. 43:16-21 and John 12:24.

Rise, O church, like Christ arisen

This eucharistic hymn was requested for the fiftieth anniversary of Lutheran Church of the Resurrection, Roseville, Minnesota. Many of the ideas expressed were inspired by J. Michael Joncas' November 1996 presentation to the Federation of Diocesan Liturgical Commissions: our identity as God's people, our choice in following the wounded Christ, the cost of such a choice.

Sweet coming for which we long

The three comings of Advent: in the Christ child, in the sacramental meal, in the completion of all things.

Teach us to seek

Written during the Gulf War, this prayer for peace explores the roots of compassionate and peaceful existence by examining the life of Jesus Christ.

The journey was chosen

Gloria Dei Lutheran Church, St. Paul, Minnesota, commissioned this hymn for the ordination anniversaries of its pastors Susan Peterson and John Manz. The reflection on the baptismal journey of vocation is based on Rom. 6:11,13; 1 Kings 19:7; 1 Peter 2:9; and Isa. 55:1.

We sing the one God

This hymnic study of the church in the context of the entire history of earth, as part of a long procession journeying in the promises of God, refers to Gen. 1; Exod. 13:21-22; Gen. 15:5; and Acts 2:1-4.

SCRIPTURE REFERENCES

Genesis

1	*We sing the one God*
12:2	*A ram's horn blasting barren hills*
15:5	*We sing the one God*
15:12	*O sacred River*

Exodus

3:1–8b, 10–15	*In the desert, on God's mountain*
3:5	*In sacred manner*
13:21-22	*We sing the one God*

Numbers

24:17	*As the dark awaits the dawn*

Deuteronomy

5:22-23	*O sacred River*

1 Samuel

16:15	*A ram's horn blasting barren hills*

1 Kings

19:7	*The journey was chosen*

2 Chronicles

5:12-13	*A ram's horn blasting barren hills*

Job

12:7	*In sacred manner*
38:7	*A ram's horn blasting barren hills*

Psalms

1:3	*O sacred River*
19:1	*In sacred manner*
27:4	*O sacred River*
30:5	*In deepest night*
42:8	*In deepest night*
46:4	*O sacred River*
65:2	*In deepest night*
96:6	*O sacred River*
96:12	*In sacred manner*
137	*In deepest night*

Ecclesiastes

1:7	*O Sea, mystic Source*

Isaiah

16:9	*In deepest night*
25:6	*O sacred River*
42:3	*In deepest night*
43:1-2	*In deepest night*
43:16-21	*Rich in promise*
53:3-4	*In deepest night*
55:1	*The journey was chosen*
55:10	*O Sea, mystic Source*

Malachi
    4:2   *As the dark awaits the dawn*

Matthew
    28:1–10   *In the fair morning*

Mark
    14:3–9   *Holy woman, graceful giver*
    14:34   *In deepest night*

Luke
    14:12–13, 24   *O sacred River*
    24:1–7   *In the fair morning*
    24:13–35   *Day of arising*
    24:28–35   *Blessing be and glory*

John
    11:35   *In deepest night*
    12:24   *Rich in promise*
    15:5   *O blessed spring*
    20:19–31   *Rise, O church, like Christ arisen*
    21:9–14   *Blessing be and glory*

Acts
    2:1–4   *We sing the one God*

Romans
    6:3–9   *Christ is the life*
    6:11,13   *The journey was chosen*
    14:8   *Christ is the life*

Colossians
    1:15–20   *Christ, burning Wisdom*
    3:12–16   *Beloved, God's chosen*

Hebrews
    1:3   *As the dark awaits the dawn*

1 Peter
    2:9   *The journey was chosen*

2 Peter
    1:19   *As the dark awaits the dawn*

Revelation
    7:12   *Blessing be and glory*
    22:1–4   *O Sea, mystic Source*
    22:16   *As the dark awaits the dawn*

TOPICAL INDEX

TUNE INDEXES

COMPOSER INDEX

ACKNOWLEDGEMENTS

I have many people to thank who have helped me on this road. Among them are:

My parents, Myrtle Palo and the late John W. Palo
"Vicar" Martin Lundi, children's choir director
Robert Potts, fifth grade teacher
Helen Dickey, junior high music teacher
Frederick Jackisch, director of music, Wittenberg Chapel
Ken Elkin, church musician, friend
J. Arthur Faber, English professor
Trudy Faber, organ professor
Margret Kommel, voice professor
St. Benet's Bookstore, Chicago, where I first found Merton
Jerry Aman, SJ, friend and raiser of the dead
Carlo Palo, uncle and encourager
Martin Behrmann, conductor
Irmgard Hartmann–Dressler, voice professor
Ray and Jan Lester, friends and spiritual guides
Jan Bowman, friend, who encouraged me to write
Mary Virginia Micka, poet
Bill Hill, philosophy professor
Blanche Marie Gallagher, BVM, artist
Michael Fortune, professor
Stephen Schmidt, religion professor
Martin Seltz, editor and risk-taker
My family
My friends
My colleagues
David

The danger with such a list is, of course, that all the people who have blessed my life have in some way contributed to who I am, and thus, to how and what I write. I have tried to mention those who had either a particular influence on the areas of music, church music, poetry, and the arts in spiritual life, or who, by a specific enlightening or encouraging word to me, helped me find my way. I'm sure I will slap my forehead when I think of others I should have named. You know, I hope, who you are and will, I pray, forgive. I am indebted to all of you. ~ *Susan Palo Cherwien*

ABOUT THE AUTHOR

Susan Palo Cherwien was born in 1953 in Ashtabula, Ohio, where she was generously exposed to the music and poetry of the Christian tradition at Zion Evangelical Lutheran Church. She was especially influenced by her time in the children's choir, directed by Vicar Martin Lundi, who assigned her first solo—in Finnish. Susan began writing poetry in grade school, and continued throughout her adolescent years and into her time at Wittenberg University, where she studied church music and vocal performance. In her junior year she attended the Berliner Kirchenmusikschule, and then returned to Berlin to study voice from 1976-1981 after graduating from Wittenberg.

Not until 1987 did she begin to combine her passion for music, poetry, and spirituality in the composing of hymn texts. In 1993 Susan completed a master's degree in Liberal Studies at Mundelein College, Chicago, where she focused on spirituality, ritual, and the arts. She lives in St. Louis Park, Minnesota with her spouse David and sons Jeremiah and Benjamin.